POET
IN OUR
MIDST

Raymond Hartmann

To order additional copies of this book, contact:
Xlibris
844-714-8691
www.Xlibris.com
Orders@Xlibris.com

ISBN: Softcover   978-1-4500-6041-7
        EBook   978-1-6641-6560-1

Print information available on the last page

Rev. date: 05/17/2021

The MUSE dwells in the subconscious accumulating and processing all experience. The MUSE plays the role of creator of much art, music and poetry. When the conscious mind is open, the MUSE gushes to the surface exposing its creation often without special effort by the writer.

Many of the poems in "Poet in our Midst" came about in this manner. The poems were influenced by a variety of experiences amongst family, friends, acquaintances or events. They are humorous, romantic, philosophical and political expressions that are part of my life. The writing of these poems has been a journey that I wish to share with you, the reader. I trust while reading them you will be entertained, enlightened and inspired. Thank you for peering into my inner-sanctum, I urge you to peer into your own.

"A TALL Tale"

This is a story – it's about my adventure
I know you'll enjoy it – that is my conjecture

I was born in a barn – at the age of five
I had built it myself – golly, sakes alive

I was the youngest – there were twelve siblings
I became their leader – cuz I knew of all things

Daddy packed us into a wagon – we headed out west
As exciting journeys go – this was the best

Going past the plains – people occupying the land
They didn't much like us – they came with a band

We circled our wagon – it was seventy feet long
We had realized immediately – something was wrong

I snatched up their missiles – right out of the air
I returned their fire – it gave them a scare

Next came the mountains – we crossed them on high
It was cold as the devil – I thought we would die

We reached California – the place we would stay
We were very exhausted – from a tiring day

In a beautiful valley – we planted the vines
After the harvest – we produced many wines

The 'Nectar of the Gods' – we drank every drop
Then we all went on welfare – our long journey a flop

Verse by: 'Ramon the Poet' – December 2007
www.mnartists.org/raymond_hartmann

"Ripe Old Age"

If it is your desire –
To live to a 'Ripe Old Age'
You must go through the chapters –
Live them page-by-page

First, there is your childhood –
Not easy as you may think
You must become socialized –
Adapt or you will sink

There are many illness' –
You might catch the flu
The dangers of the playground –
Be aware of every clue

Next you become a young adult –
Get through those teenage years
It can be an awkward time –
And bring on many tears

When you reach majority –
Live past twenty-one
There are skills to master -
Can't stroll, you must run

The trials you must endure –
Throughout your working life
You must bring home the bacon –
Perhaps a family and a wife

You may have achieved success –
Moved into your middle years
Many challenges survived –
Put you through all the gears

Grandchildren and retirement –
Now enjoy those 'Golden Years'
The competition never ends –
You must keep up with your peers

It's not easy growing old –
You really must be tough
The aches and pains you now feel –
At times are very rough

You've past through all the stress –
On the cusp of the 'Ripe Old Age'
Congratulations are in order –
Still here on life's grand stage

Perhaps it's time for more travel –
Since you've downsized your home
It's time to visit near and far –
Grand adventures when you roam

Once you reach that 'Ripe Old Age' –
Passed life's every test
Coping with your senior maladies –
You now deserve a rest

When come your final years –
On your past you dwell
Your futures all behind you –
We trust you've lived it well

Yes, the future is all behind –
On the downward slope of the hill
Whatever lies ahead now –
Only time will tell

Verse by: 'Ramon the Poet'
www.mnartists.org/raymond_hartmann

"The Club"

Out on the street – you'll take many chances
Careful, stay alert – make no sideway glances

It is treacherous out there – a lot going on
If you are not with it – you soon will be gone

It is tough on the street – you got limited choices
You can't be too watchful – hear the right voices

If you want a good life – stay away from the jive
There's an alternate way – that'll keep you alive

Come, join the Club – it's your best opportunity
Be mentored and coached – in positive activity

Stay on the street – get crazy in the head
Chuckin' and Jivin' – not long you'll be dead

So, listen up now – get rid of the hate
Get on the right path – life can be great

Come, join the Club – it's for Boys and for Girls
Become successful – turn ashes to pearls

Come, join the Club – like many before you
Young men and young women – you will become too

Come, join the Club – there's a location nearby
If you hadn't already – you'll be wondering why

**The Boys and Girls Club of the Twin Cities
verse by: 'Ramon the Poet'
www.mnartists.org/Raymond_hartmann**

"LIFE"

LIFE IS LIKE AN OCEAN RIDE –
WE COME AND GO UPON ITS TIDE

AT TIMES LIFE CAN BE VERY STORMY –
OTHER TIMES SERENE AND CALM

HAVE SOME LIFELINES NEAR AS CAN –
SO YOU CAN HELP YOUR FELLOW MAN

REACHOUT TO THOSE HAD THINGS GO WRONG –
KEEP YOUR STATION TRUE AND STRONG

STAY ON A STEADY COURSE THE WHILE –
AND THOSE AROUND WILL KEEP A SMILE

WHEN YOUR JOURNEY COMES TO THE END
WITH MEMORIES OF DEEDS WELL DONE –
ACT UPON YOUR SOUL A SOOTHING BALM

R. G. "Ramon the Poet" HARTMANN
JANUARY 2006

"Therapy"

There's Carol and Lana – occasionally Eve
They do things to your body – that are hard to believe

Techniques they use – are really a scream
Carol explains it – she's the Analogy Queen

Twisted, contorted – you feel like a clown
You're put into positions – turned upside down

Twisted, contorted – pulled by your head
They jump on your body – your face turns bright red

Twisted, contorted – still don't understand
They're trying to cure you – it's all done by hand

Twisted, contorted – squashed like a bug
Treatment is over – Lana gives me my hug

Slouching and slumping – I walk that way
Sitting or sleeping – that's how I stay

When totally stretched out – the way that I should
Everything will be better – that'll be good

Some day when it's over – and I'm finally cured
No more twisting, contorting – I give you my word

Give me a discharge – say that I'm well
If that ever happens – I'll be happy as Hell

Verse by: 'Ramon the Poet' February 2006

5

"The Wine Dinner"

The wines this night – Italiano
We're enjoying them – at Maggiano

Some of the wines – fermented twice
We all agree – they go down nice

The Vintner sez – you like or no
We really care – we're in the know

The fare is great – satisfies our palate
We're living big – drinking wine a lot

We love the wine – we love to eat
This evening's time – cannot be beat

You'll love this place – it just takes once
The congenial staff – the ambiance

So, whenever you – seek great cuisine
Just remember that – Maggiano is the scene

Verse by: 'Ramon the Poet'
www.mnartists.org/raymond_hartmann

"Speak only Good"

Slashes and blows – hurt flesh and bone
Ill spoken words – pierce the unknown
Attacks and sleights – slice to the soul
Leave in its wake – a gaping hole

The inner feelings – which run deep
Hold the resentments – there we keep
Fragile emotions – we cannot hide
Damaged egos – destroy our pride

Since we are sensitive – always be kind
Every reassurance – will ease the mind
Don't cast aspersions – speak only good
Think it through – as you should

It's best to wear – a smiley face
Helps make the world – a happy place
That is the way – to get along
Then we will fill – our hearts with song

Verse by: 'Ramon the Poet'

"Who We Are"

Do we know who we are
As our eye distorts the mirror
Are we truly on the level
As we handle life and career

Personality split down the middle
Flitting from one side to the other
Is it possible to recognize one's self
While we judge sister and brother

We may be equivocal deep down
But never admit any wrong
We need to keep our esteem
As we sell our soul for the song

All the hurt and the damage
Created by things that we say
Let us pray for a change of heart
Let our mind be clear as day

Take the path to higher ground
Put anger and prejudice aside
Then we will know fulfillment
Truth and peace will abide

Verse by: 'Ramon the Poet'
www.mnartists.org/raymond_hartmann

"Forevermore"

Our pilgrimage here on earth -
With many souls that come and go
It is a time for grand adventure -
As we mature and grow

Family and community is -
How we experience life
We learn how to cope with it -
Occasionally laced with strife

But most of all it is our friends -
We enjoy as we grow old
Socializing we most highly prize -
The gift that's solid gold

Suddenly, things don't go quite well -
Then there comes the day
We get the news we dread to hear -
We can no longer stay

So there is nothing I can say -
To let my feelings show
Exactly what the situation is -
We both already know

The days, the years, the time gone by -
With you my wonderful friend
The companionship, the memories -
Have been a heaven send

I am still here for your support -
To let you know I care
That this time together yet -
So precious and aware

Too soon it seems now -
We must part
There will always be for you -
A special place in my heart

As your journey here on earth -
Nears to its conclusion
Take note of all accomplishment -
With pride and satisfaction

So my dear buddy, my famous pal -
Before that final adieu
Remember all that we have shared -
And my great love for you

Verse by: 'Ramon the Poet'

9

'BLISS'

Wonderful BLISS - a euphoric state of mind

Creating beautiful feelings - like no other kind

What happens when bliss - begins to wane

Everything in chaos - it'll drive you insane

BLISS is but ignorance - does not include facts

Keeps your mind in a cloud - that's how it acts

BLISS keeps us distracted - everything is good

Examine, be open - is what we should

Check out the evidence - get in the know

Become enlightened - to the bad seeds we sow

If you do nothing - but stand on the side

You'll not be ready - for the terrible slide

BLISS is but ignorance - it is not real

You're in a cloud - while your wealth they steal

Wake up! smell the toxins - so you won't regret

Letting things get so bad - you'll never forget

Now is the time - you must take a stand

Get rid of the toxins - take pride in our land

If you remain selfish - and are not concerned

When things collapse - you'll get what you've earned

Once things are broken - all fallen apart

It is very difficult - to repair your heart

Remember that prevention - is worth more than cure

It is proactive attention - we need to insure

BLISS is but ignorance - please understand

Things crumbling, breaking - across the land

Dangerous waters - the deep end of the pool

Take action, get going - don't be a fool

You'll be Blissfully happy - once things aright

But, it won't happen - without a fierce fight

Involvement and courage - are much overdue

Wake up! Smell the toxins - now it's all up to you

Verse by: 'Ramon the Poet'

www.mnartists.org/raymond_hartmann

'The Cure'

Now I'm in the hands of the Medicos –
They are working on a cure
The treatments are not quite so bad –
As side effects I endure

Bed sores, mouth sores and acid reflux –
I cannot count them out
Radiation, Chemotherapy –
And now I've got the gout

The nurses come in frequently –
With needles and such things
Amongst the many issues –
That my illness brings

Confined here in the Hospital –
With hopes results are good
Anxious for the moment –
I get back to my neighborhood

Until that time is come –
And I'm back on the job
I'm gonna make the best of it –
My good spirits they cannot rob

I will tough it out –
Come through with colors flying
I will be good as new again –
My heart, body and soul aringing

Verse by: 'Ramon the Poet"
www.mnartists.org/raymond_hartmann

"Jazz88 at Duplex"

The cuisine is gourmet
Paired with Alexis Bailley wine
Featuring four courses
The preparations are divine

New French Bakery baguette
Accompanies the lentil soup
The wine, Rose Noir
Matching flavors are a coup

Haddock and house made sausage
Spinach, risotto and red pepper
With Seyval Blanc for wine
A delight for all to remember

Braised Broccolini and Parsnip
Blueberry demi-glace on Quail
The wine, of course, Voyageur
Wonderful flavors that avail

Grasshopper cheesecake
A perfect dessert delight
With superb Chocolate Port
A finishing touch just right

Musical accompaniment
Provided by Robert Bell
Sonja Hayden and her staff
Performed exceptionally well

Kevin Barnes and Nan Bailley
Co-hosts of the event
Food, wine and camaraderie
An evening most pleasant

Verse by: Ramon the poet
January 20, 2010

"Ode to Mothers"

Here's to the Mothers –
We salute one and all
They raise the children –
They help them stand tall

Here's to the Mothers –
They cook, clean and sew
They toil long hours –
That we all know

Here's to the Mothers –
They're the family glue
They dote on the Kinder –
The Kinder love you

Young Mothers, Single Mothers –
All are adored
Grandmothers, Stepmothers –
All in accord

Here's to the families –
Who make Mothers proud
Here's to sons and daughters –
Who praise them aloud

Wishes for a Mothers Day –
Filled with much cheer
Then go on mothering –
Through-out the year

Verse by: 'Ramon the Poet'
May 10, 2009

"government issue"

Honor, Duty, Country - all in the scope of our mission
A standard of conduct - under any condition

Serving in the military - Army, Air Force, Navy, Marines
You'll soon find out - just what that means

It's five in the morning - get up, hit the floor
Jump into your boots - get out the door

Out of the sack - up on your feet
Assemble immediately - in the company street

March to the range - fire your 'GUN'
Then on to the bivouac - a five-mile run

That's how you train - it's done everyday
If you can't lead - get out of the way

They treat you real harsh - to see how you'll act
You're whipped into shape - that is a fact

Worked to exhaustion - then do it some more
They rework your psyche - to prepare you for war

We fill the ranks for - Army, Air force, Navy, Marines
Ready, willing and able - well oiled machines

The home of the brave - the land of the free
Now we are ready - to defend the country

We are Americans - Red, White and Blue
Protecting Democracy - and friends who are true

We are the GI's - we are standing tall
God bless America - God bless us all

Verse by 'Ramon the Poet' - October 2008
www.mnartists.org/raymond_hartmann

"Friends"

Friendship like your family —
A gift so very special
Support when you need it —
Or any time at all

Friends are there to listen —
You can tell them how you feel
That is why they are so crucial —
To keep an even keel

Old friends are always there —
Standing by year after year
The messages they bring —
To boost our happiness and cheer

So, thank you for being friends —
O'er the time that has gone past
We cherish all you've given —
We shall be best friends that last

Verse by: Ramon the Poet
www.mnartists.org/raymond_hartmann

"Casualties of War"

When the soldier falls –
And a life is lost
The supreme sacrifice –
The ultimate cost

Hence fulfilled the duty –
Went to meet the call
Each one of them killed –
Surely affects us all

The loss of a comrade –
Has a strong impact
On the surviving troops –
That is a cold, hard fact

A frequent occurrence, death –
Which goes on day after day
Every battle, every skirmish –
Death does not go away

The remains are always handled –
With very special care
Transported to a haven –
Then readied to repair

Cleaned up, put back together –
As well as one can expect
A Fresh dress uniform –
Every detail is correct

A soldier escort is assigned –
For the long journey home
With great honor and respect –
The fallen never left alone

Friends and community –
Show support and feel so bad
Family and loved ones, however –
Feel proud and yet so sad

Another flag draped casket –
Displayed with "Old Glory"
Many died already, many will die yet –
In this endless, horrid story

Verse by: 'Ramon the Poet'

"the TRUTH"

To tell you the TRUTH – a phrase often used
Much of the time – it is being abused

I am honest and truthful – the liar will pose
In the light of day – his lies will expose

The truth is self-evident – it is not a lie
It goes without saying – you'll know bye and bye

One telling how righteous – while making a plea
Be alert and be cautious – you should most likely flee

Telling stories and fables – they try to confound
In the final analysis – they'll be no longer around

Keep your mind open – however, use care
Examine very thoroughly – make sure it is fair

The truth is very simple – not wrapped in a web
The truth is straightforward – does not cloud your head

Seek always the truth – for come what may
The truth shall prevail – at the end of the day

Verse by: 'Ramon the Poet'
www.mnartists.org/raymond_hartmann

-- My Little Pillow --

My little pillow – is all filled with beads
Don't know what's in it – tho' it fulfills my needs

I always have it with me – I use it all the time
It feels so good – it is comfort sublime

Although you may think it – I'm not really lazy
My pillow is fantastic – I know it sounds crazy

It is so relaxing – it eases the pain
If I should ever lose it – I'd replace it again

Some people have 'Blankies' – which are their crutch
I have my beaded pillow – I love it so much

While using the pillow – I'm in my glory
I'll never be without it – that's my pillow story

So if you doubt me – it won't make me cry
The only way to find out – give one a try

I'll tell you once more – then I'll put it to rest
My beaded little pillow – is simply the best

R. G. 'Ramon' Hartmann   April 2008

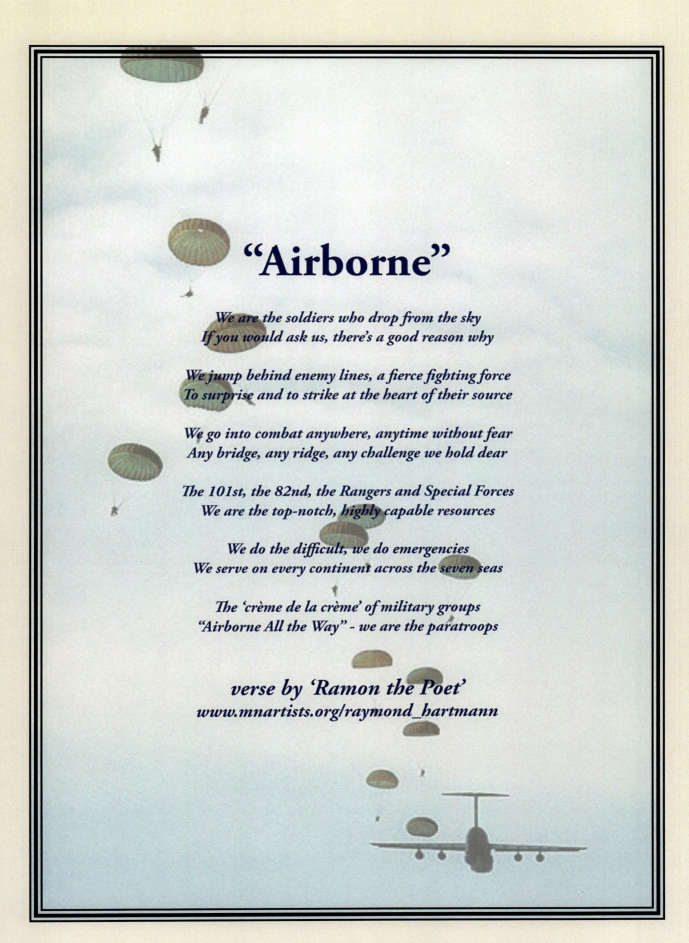

"Airborne"

We are the soldiers who drop from the sky
If you would ask us, there's a good reason why

We jump behind enemy lines, a fierce fighting force
To surprise and to strike at the heart of their source

We go into combat anywhere, anytime without fear
Any bridge, any ridge, any challenge we hold dear

The 101st, the 82nd, the Rangers and Special Forces
We are the top-notch, highly capable resources

We do the difficult, we do emergencies
We serve on every continent across the seven seas

The 'crème de la crème' of military groups
"Airborne All the Way" - we are the paratroops

verse by 'Ramon the Poet'
www.mnartists.org/raymond_hartmann

"Oh, My Aching Back"

We walk on our hind legs – Homo Erectus
An eloquent idea, but – it did not perfect us

Bulging discs, Stenosis – and Spondylolisthesis
A major flaw in design – of the human species

We have many aches and pains – feeling very sore
Sitting, walking, standing hurts – even opening a door

We go to the Ortho Doc – to see how we can heal
X-rays, CT Scans, MRI's – then operate is the deal

First insert steel rods – onto the spine
Straighten up the vertebrae – get 'em into line

Next comes recovery – you rehabilitate
Do your Physical Therapy – lift lots of weight

We've been there also – we do empathize
You must make an effort now – you do realize

We pray that you – improve more every day
You'll be dancing soon – we just want to say

Verse by: 'Ramon the Poet'

"Love is Forever"

I lie here beside you
All comfy in bed
Holding you closely
Loving thoughts in my head

Dreams of the future
Remembering the past
I lie here and wonder
How long does love last

The good times we've shared
The many years spent together
Lo, we shall never part
For our love is forever

How long does love last
Love is forever
How long does love last
Forever and ever

Verse by: 'Ramon the Poet'
www.mnartists.org/raymond_hartmann

"You Must Not Quit"

When things go wrong – as they often will
the path you're on – seems all up hill

When funds are low – and debts are high
you'd like to smile – but instead you sigh

When problems are there – pressing down a bit
rest a little while – but do not quit

Life is sometimes strange – it will twist and turn
as everyone will – soon enough learn

Many a failure – can be turned about
in order to survive – you must stick it out

Success is failure – turned inside out
there is a silver lining – in the clouds of doubt

You may never know – how close you are
results may be near – though seem so far

So stick to the task – when you're hardest hit
when things seem worst – you must not quit

Verse by: 'Ramon the Poet'
www.mnartists.org/raymond_hartmann

"Jaguar Automobiles"

A marque incomparable – a grand history
A symbol of excellence – most fashionably
Mercedes and Lexus – they look much the same
Chrysler and Lincoln – are really quite tame

Audi and BMW – very nice wheels
Toyota and Nissan – right on their heels
Lots of good cars – all very similar
None like Jaguar – it's much better by far

While drivin' round town – in your Jaguar
You can be confident – they'll know who you are
Great looks and luxury – a real work of art
Owning a Jaguar – is really smart

Jags are outstanding – as they come down the street
Driving the X's – you're amongst the elite
To the theater – or just out to dine
Arrive in a Jaguar – a motorcar that's so fine

The choice is narrow – if you want the best
Show up in a Jaguar – stand out from the rest
It's all up to you – now you decide
Do you want transportation – or a really great ride

Verse by: Ramon the Poet
At: mnartists.org/Raymond_hartmann

'Social Conduct'

How should we live – how shall we behave
What model to keep – from cradle to grave

The way that we act – while out on the street
Just stay within bounds – so life will be sweet

We must follow the rules – because otherwise
The village around – will cut down your size

The church and the school – help guide your way
Teaching 'Moral Conduct' – they hold much sway

But as you mature – you will soon see
The key to it all – is your family

Your mother, your father – also friends and siblings
Create the mode – how you handle things

Sports, theatre and the arts – have great appeal
They provide ways to express – just how you feel

Achieve self-respect – that, you should desire
You can become one – whom people admire

Enjoy success in life – whatever you do
So, you decide – it's all up to you

Verse by: 'Ramon the Poet'

"The Grand Deception"

William Jefferson Clinton - number Forty One
An interesting character - a real son-of-a-gun
Called 'Slick Willy' - and various other names
Very well deserved - he played lots of games

Off to a great start - everything went quite well
Then Monica and the blue dress - it went flying down hill
Playing words and twisting logic - refusing to confess
Hillary and Chelsea - stood by him none the less

Most all were satisfied - many conservatives were not
Because of indiscretions - the Oval Office was very hot
Clinton was impeached - for lying about the girls
Put on a sidetrack - while his presidency unfurls

A stain on his legacy - otherwise quite good
A surplus and strong economy - all misunderstood
The end of his era - it was very abrupt
Leaving that high office - his reputation left bankrupt

George Walter Bush - number forty two
Son of number forty - 'W' we hardly knew
Coming out of Texas - Governor of the state
Brought along Dick Cheney - as his running mate

Talking really BIG TALK - in Texas style
Large promises, euphoria - for only a short while
It did not take long - before it wore real thin
They brought on the war - no one will ever win

Setting up good friends - with enormous gain
Handing out contracts - would create the pain
Bush, Cheney, Rumsfeld - several others too
For many evil deeds - the Devil get his due

Eight disastrous years - the economy in shambles
Allegedly a healer - but took preposterous gambles
The voters said enough - we'll have no more of that
Went to the polls in numbers - put in a Democrat

Barack Hussein Obama - number forty four
Will he be any different - or just another bore
Bailing out Wall Street - to save the economy
More debt accumulation - we go further up a tree

Now we're buying business - Chrysler and GM
Nationalize the banks - where will it ever end
Set for One World Order - it is coming fast
America the Beautiful - is it a thing of the past

Verse by: 'Ramon the Poet'

"Frog in my Shoe"

I was in the garage - getting ready for a chore
Put on my pants - my work shoes on the floor

I picked up my shoes - something wasn't right
Some kinda' creature - in there just outa' sight

Ah, there it is - what a surprise
A shy little frog - nearly met his demise

I took it in my palm - headed down to the shore
Set it gently in the lake - don't come back anymore

It kept frog kicking - as it swam on its way
I went back to work - the frog saved this day

The moral of the story - at least, how I see it
Look before you leap - your shoe may not fit

Verse by: 'Ramon the Poet'

26

--PAIN--
The Invisible Burden

I meet them at the doctors
Or at the therapist
I never knew the pain they're in
Nor how much life they've missed

You will never know how much
I know I never knew
You cannot understand despair
Until it happens to you

You cannot know the way they feel
And every day's concession
No longer doing things they loved
Nor fathom their depression

Myself, I know now what they feel
The nagging horrible pain
Pain that's with you constantly
You struggle with routine

Trying hard to carry on
To do the best I'm willing
Combating pain day-in day-out
A challenge overwhelming

I never seem to have a hope
That things will get much better
It's an effort to keep spirits up
And not becoming bitter

Verse by: Ramon the Poet

"Blue Sky"

The Brooklyn Bridge –
Florida swampland
An opportunity waits –
Got the deed right in hand

They're really great deals –
It is absolutely true
You are my friend –
I'll take care of you

Madoff, Petters, many others –
We were just misunderstood
Why'd they hafta interfere –
We were doing really good

Right here in our hearts –
We've got your best interest
You'll make lotsa moola –
If you want to invest

If you desire a nice home –
Just go to the bank
Borrow all that you can –
Before you go in the tank

Don't worry about a thing –
Everything is just fine
If any tough queries –
Just hand them a line

Get everything you want –
You deserve the prize
When it all falls apart –
Oh My! What a surprise

Then there's the government –
They're here to serve
If you don't cooperate –
You've got lotsa nerve

What ever goes wrong –
Give us a shout
We'll lend you a hand –
A taxpayer bailout

Ponzi schemes are a symptom –
There's disease at the core
Fiat currency, Fractional banking –
Greed and corruption will soar

So, there you have it –
Now you know why
World-Wide expansion –
We all got "Blue Sky"

Two-Way Talkin'

Although I like the teacher
The teacher wants to talk and talk
Some students no longer listen
Others just want to walk

If teacher only understood
We have a lot to say
Our achievement would improve
If communications were two-way

There must be Two-Way Talkin'
The students must be heard
Without Two-Way Talkin'
The classroom becomes absurd

Instead of being bored
We could get much more done
Learning would be more effective
Our education would be fun

So, let's all get together
Work on the same page
With changes for the better
Education comes of age

Verse by: Ramon the Poet

www.mnartists.org/raymond_hartmann

"....the Boiling point"

Add some oil to the water –
Place the FROG in the pot
The FROG is indifferent –
The water is not yet hot

Turn on the burner –
It's starting to get warm
The FROG doesn't notice –
Because it seems the norm

Eventually it boils –
The FROG is now dead
It came on so gradual –
Didn't know what lay ahead

Now the people do not realize –
We are in the same game
It is getting extremely hot –
Our economy is lame

Stored value and labor –
Have been depreciated
By an unscrupulous system –
Dire circumstances created

The US Dollar was debauched –
Fiat currency led to inflation
Free Enterprise has passed –
We have ruined our great nation

We are at the Boiling Point –
It is now 'Do-or-Die'
Checks & Balances gone missing –
The END GAME is nearby

The people must WAKE UP! –
The Congress brought in hand
Throw off the chains that bind –
God save our sovereign land

Verse by: 'Ramon the Poet'
www.mnartists.org/raymond_hartmann

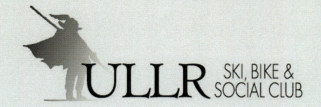

ULLR SKI, BIKE & SOCIAL CLUB

What the heck is ULLR
Nordic God or beast
Is ULLR still mythology
No, not in the least

Skiing, biking, partying
You'll always have a voice
Participate in all events
With ULLR there's a choice

What is ULLR now
A person or a group
ULLR now is both
That is the scoop

ULLRs are doing something good
Most every day
We are charitable and cheerful
That is the ULLRs' way

But, what is an ULLR
Is it a Gal or is it a Guy
ULLR is androgynous
Please, don't ask me why

ULLR has a charity
It's called the Foundation
Raising funds for those in need
The Gala Dinner's a sensation

So, tell me then exactly
What does an ULLR do
ULLR does a lot of things
Some familiar, some are new

We are singles, or we're couples
Getting together happily
More than just a social club
We are an ULLR family

ULLR provides activities
To keep you in the mix
Sports and trips, social events
There are many picks

There is an ULLR Board
That directs the group
Winter, Spring, Summer, Fall
They'll keep you in the loop

ULLRs do go schussing
Down the mountain side
ULLRs do go biking too
Because they like to ride

So, what is the ULLR
A group of folks that do not fuss
Put some spice into your life
Com'on and join with us

Verse by: 'Ramon the Poet'

"NEUROPATHY"

Neuropathy – Neuropathy
It gets on my nerves
The numbness, the burning
Something nobody deserves

Neuropathy – Neuropathy
It gives me much pain
The tingling, the aching
Nearly drives me insane

While sitting or lying
Feet and legs are on fire
Intensely uncomfortable
It's like a hot wire

Restless and turning
I can't sleep at night
It doesn't get better
The tunnel's end has no light

Stumbling and staggering
That's how I walk now you see
If you should watch me
I'm sure you'll agree

Neuropathy – Neuropathy
It gives me dismay
Unbearable suffering
Please go away

Verse by: 'Ramon the Poet'

Valentine

Valentines Day comes just once a year
You fill my life with hope and good cheer

This Valentines Day I pledge you my love
You are my Angel sent from above

You're my Valentine day in and day out
The love that binds us is what it's about

My love for you grows with each passing year
I'm thankful always, for our time is so dear

Everything is swell when we are together
Here's to our love, Valentines forever

'Ramon the Poet'

My Fault

Not being perfect - I am fallible
For my mistakes - I am liable
Using poor judgment - time and again
It is only human - that is my spin

I feel so badly - I was immature
I'm trying to change - that I assure
For my behavior - I'm filled with guilt
A sword in my heart - up to the hilt

My fault, my fault - my most grievous fault
The pain, the conscience - when will it halt
Error after error - time after time
The irony of it - is so sublime

My fault, my fault - my most grievous fault
I need this agony - to come to a halt
Whenever my actions - create such strife
I need to realize - I must change my life

My friends, my family - my acquaintances too
I beg your forgiveness - I wish to be true
With this confession - I hope to atone
For my transgressions - all damage I've done

Therefore, today - and I will be brief
Beginning right now - I will turn a new leaf
With trust and belief - new judgment I've found
I'll make this pledge - to turn my life around

Verse by: 'Ramon the Poet'

*** Return Liberty ***

Ah, sweet liberty – wherever did you go
We have lost our vision – that has brought us low

The Woodrow Wilson pact – United World Federalists
Changed a basic tenet – enabling Imperialists

So, the return of serfdom – was then brought about
We slipped back into slavery – but there is a sure way out

Dump the Federal Income Tax – that has us torn apart
It never should have happened – we were not very smart

The Congress has the right they said – to lay and collect the tax
Imposts, duties, excises – are the correct, true facts

We lost the right to privacy – in our persons, papers, things
A Constitutional violation – that very loudly rings

The founding Fathers stated – cuz they knew so very well
The mulcting of our livelihood – would cast an evil spell

Now is the opportunity – to restore Free Enterprise
We have the chance to rid ourselves – of that system we despise

The congress must acknowledge – we're in a dire situation
They must correct the error – that is bleeding our great nation

The working class and the poor – will all have much more
Everyone will benefit – our economy will soar

The time has come – the stage is set
The principles of liberty – shall again be met

HR 25, the Fair Tax Bill – is the true solution
Get back 'The American Way' – that is our resolution

Verse by: 'Ramon the Poet'
www.mnartists.org/raymond_hartmann

"On Bended Knee"

Darling, when first we met
I loved you from the start
I keep you always in my mind
I keep you always in my heart

Our time together
So precious, so dear
I am elated and joyous
Whenever you're near

My dearest, my darling
You are my one and only
Stay with me always
We will never be lonely

With solemn intentions
On bended knee
I pledge you my love
For all eternity

You and I together
The rest of our life
My dearest darling
Will you be my wife

Verse by: 'Ramon the Poet'

"Going Home"

On this fine day I'm going home –
Getting back to things I've known

Forgetting all life's stress and strife –
I'm looking forward to my new life

All the things were in my past –
Are only memories at last – at last

So now it's time to hit the trail –
Try staying here is no avail

Now everything is said and done –
It's time to leave – it's time to run

I'm satisfied this journey's over –
I go to peaceful pastures – clover

Free from all life's concern I've know –
Free at last I'm going home – I'm going home!

Verse by: 'Ramon the Poet' – 02/07/2006

"Ol' George"

He's a good Ol' Dawg -
the last one of three
Two have passed on -
they were Gus and Gracie

Poor Ol' George -
he's well past fourteen
Crippled and blind -
even deaf it would seem

Nearly a hundred now -
compared to human years
He's feeble and staggering -
nearly brings you to tears

He can no longer hold his bowels -
he can't make it outside
Around the house he makes a mess -
wherever he's at he just lets it slide

His food and his water -
are in the middle of the floor
So he can easily get to it -
because his balance is poor

He's been with us since a puppy -
just like one of the family
When he is gone at last -
we will all miss him dearly

So, when George leaves us -
we may just leave it at that
Perhaps, no more dogs -
but we'll still have a cat

Verse by: 'Ramon the Poet'

"Reunion Visions"

St. Louis Park High School -
Class of Nineteen Fifty Three
A top-notch class, one of the best -
With that we all agree

Though many years have past -
The memories held so dear
So we hold a class reunion now -
Scheduled on every fifth year

Classmates show themselves -
To be filled with curiosity
Anxious to greet old friends -
The ones they are dying to see

This one is the fifty-fifth -
The year two thousand eight
Our median age is seventy-three -
Time now is getting late

Some amongst us have graying hair -
Others are a little bit balding
You merely have to glance around -
To note we are more than surviving

Mostly though we are aging well -
We're still 'Fit as a Fiddle'
A little wrinkle here and there -
Extra weight around the middle

Successful people one and all -
Each in their own endeavor
Vanilla, chocolate, strawberry -
It's all in what you favor

Now where do we go from here -
As great challenges abound
Take action to improve our world -
Please, don't just lie around

Share your talent; share your wealth -
Give what time you can
Take on the responsibility -
To help your fellow man

The time is right; the time is now -
It's time to make a mark
Then we will all be proud to say -
We are from St. Louis Park

Verse by: 'Ramon the Poet'

"Poetic Verse"

A custom poem –
Especially for you
Whatever your need –
Any occasion I do

Memorial or wedding –
Even business mode
Birthday or Anniversary –
I will create an Ode

A Poetic Verse –
Will bring much pleasure
It is something unique –
You will always treasure

Keep portraits and videos –
Which memorialize
Add Poetic Verse –
You'll forever prize

Verse by: 'Ramon the poet'
mnartists.org/Raymond_hartmann